CONFLICT IN THE MIDDLE EAST

Dr John King

Wayland

Conflicts

Titles in the series:
Conflict in Eastern Europe
Conflict in Southern Africa
Conflict in the Middle East
The Breakup of the Soviet Union

Cover: A Kurdish guerrilla in Iraqi Kurdistan.

Title page: An Iraqi tank in Kuwait, in the aftermath of the Gulf War (March, 1991).

Picture acknowledgements
The publishers would like to thank the following for supplying their photographs for use as illustrations in this book:
Camera Press 10, 14, 17 *top* (Abbie Enock), 22, 25, 26, 27 (Karl Schumacher), 31 (*L'Express*), 35 *top*, 35 *bottom*, 38; Mary Evans Picture Library 11; Rex Features *cover* (Sipa Press/ O'Donnell), 4, 17 *bottom* (Sipa Press), 18, 20, 24 (Sipa Press), 29 (Sipa Press), 30 (Sipa Press), 33 (Sipa Press), 36 (John Reardon), 37 (John Reardon), 39 (Sipa Press), 40 (Sipa Press), 41 (Sipa Press), 44 (Sipa Press), 45 *top* (Sipa Press), 45 *bottom* (Nils Jorgensen); Topham Picture Source 5 *top* (Associated Press), 5 *bottom* (World in Colour), 8, 9 (Associated Press), 12, 13, 15, 16, 23, 32 (Associated Press), 34, 43 (Associated Press).
The maps and graphics on pages 6, 19, 21 and 42 were supplied by Peter Bull.

Series editor: William Wharfe
Editor: Margot Richardson
Designer/Typesetter: Malcolm Walker/Kudos Editorial and Design Services

First published in 1993 by
Wayland (Publishers) Ltd
61 Western Road, Hove
East Sussex BN3 1JD

British Library Cataloguing in Publication Data
King, John
   Conflict in the Middle East. – (Conflicts Series)
   I. Title II. Series
   956

ISBN 0-7502-0391-9

Printed and bound in Italy by G. Canale & C.S.p.A., Turin

Contents

INTRODUCTION

The Middle East is a flash-point in world affairs. In recent times, it has been the scene of international conflict on a vast scale. The Gulf War of 1991 began after Iraq invaded neighbouring Kuwait. A coalition of Western and Arab allies drove Iraq's army back from Kuwait in a conflict involving a million soldiers, which cost billions of dollars and monopolized the attention of the world for eight months.

The Iraqi army, forced to retreat from Kuwait at the end of the Gulf War, set fire to many of Kuwait's oil wells in a final act of destruction. Here, oil workers are shown attempting to put out a fire at one oil well – shortly after the end of the war.

The Gulf War was caused by the enormous value and importance of oil, which the world depends on for fuel. Almost two-thirds of the world's known reserves of oil are in the Gulf region, under the control of a handful of countries. Had the dispute between Iraq and Kuwait not been between two oil states, it is hard to believe the USA and the world community would have become involved. But the possession of oil by Middle Eastern states means that the world watches the Middle East carefully.

There are other issues that focus Western attention on the Middle East. The first is the dispute between Israel and the Palestinians. The Middle East peace talks, which began in 1991, were to decide whether Israel will have an exclusive right to the territory of Palestine, or whether the Palestinians will themselves have, in due course, a national home once again. Then comes the conflict between Iraq and Iran. And there is also the rise, in many Middle Eastern countries, of what the West calls Muslim

The standard of living varies greatly throughout the Middle East. (Left) An affluent Kuwaiti family shops in a well-stocked supermarket.

(Below) Refuse collection in a poor area of Cairo in Egypt.

fundamentalism: the ideas of Muslims who want to return to the basics of their religion, and apply these ideas to politics.

Of course, there are other ways of thinking about regional problems, which seem just as important to the inhabitants of the Middle East themselves. There is the question of the distribution of resources: the balance between rich and poor nations as well as rich and poor individuals is much discussed in the Middle East. The rulers of the oil states, like Saudi Arabia and Kuwait, are some of the richest people in the world. On the other hand, the working class of Egypt, for example, has a typically Third World standard of living.

It is in this way that Middle Eastern countries themselves see the question of the distribution of oil resources and oil wealth, while for the West the priority is the smooth flow of oil – a vital economic resource – from producers to Western consumers. In addition, the inhabitants of the Middle East are increasingly concerned about their supply of water, which is basically more important to them than oil.

Middle Easterners also worry about their political future, and who their rulers will be. Few people in the Middle East, outside Israel, enjoy anything approaching a democratic system. But the people of the Middle East are perhaps more concerned in the short term about dignity and freedom under the law than about democracy. They also think about how countries can modernize, without the destruction of important traditional values. And they increasingly ponder the role religion should play in a modern world.

Since the Gulf War, they also wonder how to come to terms with the power of the West to inflict, at will, defeat and humiliation on any Arab government. Finally, for most inhabitants of the Middle East, the preoccupying issues are how to lead decent lives while population grows, resources become scarcer, prices rise, and, in spite of the promises of modernization, quality of life seems harder to ensure.

SETTING THE SCENE: LANDS AND PEOPLES

Countries of the Middle East today, also showing the extent of the Ottoman Empire in 1914.

Geography

The northernmost country of the Middle East is Turkey, a country of 60 million people with an expanding economy.

Historically, the whole of the Middle East was once part of the Turkish empire, known as the Ottoman Empire. The first great Turkish conquests in the Middle East were made as long ago as the sixteenth century, when Syria, Egypt and other Arab lands came under Turkish rule. The Arab states we know today came from the breakup of the Ottoman Empire.

South of Turkey lie the Arab states, namely Syria, Lebanon, Iraq and Jordan. The fifth of this group of countries, Palestine, is now Israel, as the result of the Jewish victory in the war of 1948 and the establishment of the State of Israel by the Jewish settlers. East of Turkey lies Iran, a distinct

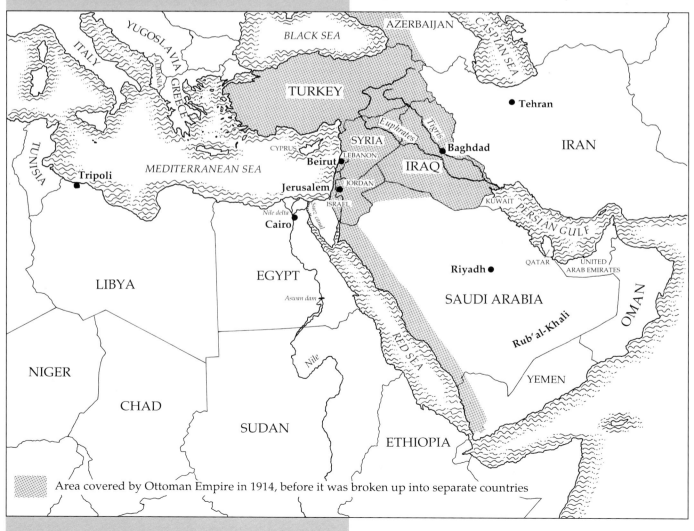

Area covered by Ottoman Empire in 1914, before it was broken up into separate countries

and non-Arabic speaking land which was never
part of the Turkish empire.

Physical geography

Much of the Middle East is desert, but there are
also great tracts of cultivated land.

Most of the Arabian Peninsula is desert, and at
its heart is the Rub' al-Khali, the empty quarter,
one of the most infertile and hostile deserts in the
world, traversed only occasionally by a handful
of Bedouin tribesmen. On the other hand Yemen,
in south-west Arabia, has cultivated hillsides
and a moderate climate.

Egypt has the fertile areas of the River Nile –
the strip of country to each side of the river, and
the delta. Densely populated and noisy, Cairo is
the largest city in the Arab world with well over
10 million inhabitants. But Egypt also has the
vast Western Desert and the stony and sterile
deserts of the Red Sea coast. To the west of
Egypt, Libya is also a desert country.

Much of the heart of Iraq and Jordan is also
desert, but the Fertile Crescent, which runs from
Lebanon round to the valleys of the Tigris and
the Euphrates in Iraq, is suitable for agriculture.
The river valleys in Iraq, the apple orchards of
Lebanon, and the fields and gardens of Syria are
rich and fertile. Turkey and Iran are partially
agricultural and partially arid.

Climate

Across the Middle East, the climate varies widely.
The blistering heat of the Arabian Peninsula and
the deserts of Egypt contrast with the more
moderate climates farther north. Even in winter
the Arabian Peninsula and Egypt are warm.
Southern Iraq and the hinterland of Jordan also
suffer fierce heat, but in Israel, Jordan and Syria
the winters can be cold. In the mountains of
northern Iraq and Iran, and eastern Turkey, where
the Kurds live, the winters can be terribly cold.

The region was one of the world's earliest
populated areas and supports a large population.
It continues to produce much of its own food.

| | Rainfall | Temperature | |
| | (average yearly, mm) | (average daily max, °C) | |
		Feb	Aug
Baghdad	137.5	18	43
Tehran	242.5	10	36
Beirut	877.5	17	32
Jerusalem	520.0	13	31
Kuwait	122.5	18	40
Cairo	27.5	21	35

The modern states

The states of the Middle East today vary widely
in their forms of political organization. Syria
and Iraq are Ba'athist regimes: in theory Arab
socialist states, but in practice autocracies. Both
rely on military strength and repression to stay
in power, and in the past each of them has relied
on the Soviet Union for outside support.

Jordan is a monarchy, tempered by an
increasingly lively parliamentary democracy.
Lebanon has a democratic framework, but is
finding its way back to stability after the long
and bruising civil war between the country's
different religious and social communities. Libya
has its own original form of government, called
the Jamahiriyyah. It is a system of popular
committees, where, in theory, the people
themselves make political decisions. In practice,
however, power remains with Libya's leader,
Colonel Gaddafi, who set up the system.

Saudi Arabia and the Gulf States are also

monarchies. In the south-west corner of Arabia, Yemen is a republic.

Egypt has its own form of presidential and parliamentary politics. Economically, capitalist free enterprise plays an increasing role, competing against a vast state sector inherited from the years when Gamal Abdel Nasser was president.

Iran is a theocratic Islamic Republic; that is, it is governed by its religious leaders. It was established on new lines by the late Ayatollah Khomeini after the fall of the Shah. Iran holds democratic elections, but has no political parties, and the important offices of state are filled by members of the clergy.

Turkey, which would like to become a member of the European Community, is working hard at modelling its society on the European democratic and social pattern. But Turkey also has important Middle Eastern links and is, in addition, bidding to be the leader of a wider Turkish-speaking community including the former Soviet Muslim Republics. Turkey is officially a secular state (not within the control of a religion), but virtually all its inhabitants are Muslim.

Israel, which also controls the Arab lands known as the Occupied Territories, is a democracy. Most of Israel's population of almost five million is now Jewish, though in Israel itself, there is an Arab minority of over 800,000 who are Israeli citizens. The one and three-quarter million people of the Occupied Territories, held by Israel since the war of 1967, are also Arabs but are not Israeli citizens, and therefore have no vote.

Economic resources

The countries of the Arabian Peninsula and the Gulf (except, up to 1992, Yemen) have, in proportion to their small populations, immense wealth based on the production of oil. These are the rich countries of the Middle East, the 'haves'. Though other countries have some oil, especially Libya and Iraq, they are, for different reasons, more aligned with the poorer countries, the 'have-nots'.

Agriculture and oil are the mainstays of the Middle Eastern economies, though Egypt, Israel and Iraq in particular have begun to develop industries. Of the states in the heart of the Middle East, Iraq has oil resources but spent much of its income on the long war it fought with Iran from 1980 to 1988. Now, after the Gulf War, Iraq faces ruin. None of the others in this group of states is rich. Israel has achieved a higher standard of living – comparable to Portugal – but relies heavily on aid from the USA.

Egypt is the Arab country with the largest population, almost 60 million. The life-blood of the country is the Nile, one of the world's great

Fishermen on Egypt's River Nile, one of the Middle East's most fertile and productive areas.

rivers. The Nile Delta is one of the world's most fertile regions, but Egypt has a growing population and faces economic difficulties. However, Egypt also receives US aid.

Peoples and religions

Except for Iran, Turkey and Israel, all the countries of the Middle East are Arabic speaking and share a common culture, based on the Arabic language and Islam. Arabs are of mixed origins, and range from the Syrians and Lebanese of broadly South European appearance to the black peoples of Sudan. Nevertheless, Arabs believe strongly that they all have much in common. The Arab culture is shared even by the minorities of Christian Arabs in Egypt, Lebanon, Syria and Iraq.

Religion is a key factor in Middle Eastern affairs. Most Arabs are Muslims, and follow the religion founded by the prophet Muhammad who died in AD 632. Muslims, like Christians, believe in one god, who is called, in Arabic, Allah. Muhammad was Allah's prophet, and the word of Allah is revealed in the Qur'an.

There are two divisions within the Muslim faith. Sunni Arabs, who are the vast majority, believe the rules of Islam are laid down in the Qur'an and by a body of traditions about what the prophet did and said in his lifetime, as well as on an agreed body of scholarly interpretation. The Sunni Muslims believe in a body of religious law as the foundation of Islam.

Shi'ites, on the other hand, believe that the leadership of the faith was passed on by the prophet's nephew and son-in-law, Ali. The Shi'ites regard themselves as the followers of Ali's spiritual descendants, and think their faith is more directly linked to the origins of Islam.

It is important not to forget that the Sunnis and Shi'ites believe what they have in common is more important than what separates them. Even though Shi'ites and Sunnis sometimes come into conflict, as in Iraq after the Gulf War, they share the basic beliefs of Islam, and in the last resort, it is with each other that Muslims feel solidarity, across any division within the faith.

Iran belongs to the Shi'ite faith but its language is Farsi, which is related to the languages of

Over 200,000 Muslim worshippers bow in prayer outside a mosque in Jerusalem's old city, which now forms part of Israel.

North India. Turks are Sunni Muslims, and speak the Turkish language. Most of the people living in the former Soviet Republics with Muslim populations speak Turkish dialects.

The Arab Christians are found in a number of countries, but the principal community is the Copts in Egypt, who make up ten per cent of Egypt's population, and are the guardians of an ancient Christian tradition. In Lebanon, half the population is Christian, and the two main communities are the Maronites and the Greek Orthodox. There are also Christians elsewhere, especially in Syria and Iraq.

Most of the Middle East's Jews are now concentrated in Israel, the Jewish state. Israel has encouraged immigration of Jews from Arab countries, and the hostility to Jews in Arab countries after 1948 also drove them out. In Morocco there remains a substantial community of perhaps 20,000 Jews, and there are a few thousand in Yemen. There are also small Jewish communities in Syria, Egypt and Turkey.

CHAPTER 3

THE FIRST WORLD WAR AND ITS RESULTS

Turkey entered the First World War on 29 October 1914. Turkey sided with Germany, which lost the war, and as a result Turkey was stripped of its Arab possessions. These territories became Syria, Iraq, Jordan and Palestine. Turkey as we know it today narrowly escaped being divided up. Only the intervention of the Turkish leader, Mustafa Kemal Ataturk, in 1919, was able to save Turkey from disintegration by rallying the Turkish people and showing the victorious Allies that Turkey would resist division.

Turkey retained the territory that became the modern Turkish state. The old Arab provinces were divided into the separate Arab countries.

The British officer, Captain TE Lawrence, who was known as Lawrence of Arabia after his success in leading Arab rebels against the Turks.

During the First World War Britain encouraged what was called the 'Arab revolt'. After the war the British tried to install the sons of the Sherif of Mecca, members of the aristocratic Hashemite family, as rulers in the Arab countries. These men and their Arab followers had fought alongside the British against the Turks in the Arab revolt, under the leadership of the British officer known as Lawrence of Arabia.

One Hashemite brother, Feisal, became King of Iraq under British protection. His brother, Abdullah, became Emir and later King of Transjordan, now the Kingdom of Jordan. The present king of Jordan, King Hussein, is King Abdullah's grandson.

The new shape of the Middle East and the boundaries between the Arab states of Syria and Iraq were settled in private agreements made between France and Britain during the war. Political arrangements were made at two international conferences: the great Paris peace conference of 1919, and the San Remo conference of 1920.

At the Paris peace conference the League of Nations was conceived. At San Remo, the Supreme Allied Council assigned mandates, authorizing Britain to take charge of Palestine and Iraq, and France to take control of Syria. The final list of countries created after the war out of former Turkish territory comprised Syria, Lebanon, Iraq, Jordan and Palestine. The mandates were confirmed by the League of Nations in 1922.

Iraq became an independent state in 1932. Syria and Lebanon were declared independent by the Free French authorities in 1941, during the Second World War. Jordan became independent in 1946.

Israel came into existence in a different way. In 1917 the British foreign secretary, Arthur Balfour, had made a promise known as the 'Balfour Declaration' to the leaders of the Jewish Zionist movement. This expressed Britain's agreement that the Jews were to be able to establish what was described as a 'national home' in Palestine.

One people which failed to gain its

The British foreign secretary in 1917, Arthur Balfour.

The Balfour Declaration

2 November, 1917. Dear Lord Rothschild, . . . I have much pleasure in conveying to you on behalf of his Majesty's Government the following declaration of sympathy with Jewish Zionist aspirations, which has been submitted to and approved by the Cabinet . . . 'His Majesty's Government views with favour the establishment in Palestine of a national home for the Jewish people, and will use its best endeavours to facilitate the achievement of this object, it being clearly understood that nothing shall be done which may prejudice the civil and religious rights of the non-Jewish communities in Palestine, or the rights and political status enjoyed by Jews in any other country.' I should be grateful if you would bring this declaration to the knowledge of the Zionist Federation . . . Yours sincerely, [signed] Arthur James Balfour.

independence during this period was the Kurds. The Kurds speak their own language and live a separate life in the mountains where Iraq, Iran and Turkey meet. They were promised an independent state called Kurdistan at the conference at San Remo. But Turkey successfully demanded that the idea of an independent Kurdistan, in what is now eastern Turkey, should be dropped. (For more on the Kurds, see Chapter 18, pages 40–1.)

Elsewhere in the Middle East new nations were also coming into being. Egypt had been independent in all but name from the old Ottoman Empire since 1805, when the great Egyptian, Khedive Muhammad Ali, took power. Britain had exercised a strong influence in Egypt since 1882 when British troops were sent to Egypt, and during the First World War when Egypt became a British protectorate. Egypt became independent in 1922, though Britain kept control of some aspects of Egyptian affairs. The last king of Egypt, King Farouk, a distant descendant of Muhammad Ali, was deposed by the Egyptian revolution of Colonel Nasser and General Neguib in 1952, which we shall read about in Chapter 6, pages 16–17.

Libya was another far flung and semi-independent region of the Ottoman Empire until 1911, when it was invaded by Italy. Libya was occupied by the Italians until after the Second World War, and it finally became fully independent in 1951.

Also around 1911, the so-called Wahhabi group gained control over most of the Arabian Peninsula, which became the independent state of Saudi Arabia in 1932. During the 1930s, the boundaries of the independent Emirates, which are today's Gulf states, were settled under British protection. The old state of Yemen in south-west Arabia signed a frontier agreement with the Saudis in 1934. The British held South Yemen as a colony. It did not become independent until 1967 (when it followed Marxist policies), and it merged with North Yemen in 1990.

Lastly, to the east, Iran was already an independent state, though foreign troops intervened in Iranian territory during the First World War. In the nineteenth century, and up to the First World War, Iran was ruled by shahs of the Qajar dynasty. After the war, there was a period of political trouble, and in 1925 the late Shah's father, a soldier, took the throne. That dynasty was not overthrown until 1979, when the Islamic Republic of Iran was set up (see Chapter 13, page 30).

CHAPTER 4

THE SECOND WORLD WAR AND ARAB NATIONALISM

The Second World War, which began in September 1939, inevitably spread to the Middle East. When Germany defeated Britain in Europe, in 1940, the British still held Egypt, the defence of which was vital. At the battle of El Alamein on 23 October 1942 a British army prevented the Germans from entering Egypt from Libya. This was the most important date of the war in the Middle East, because afterwards the tide of war began to turn in Britain's favour.

The French war-time colonial government in Syria decided to co-operate with the so-called Vichy regime – a provisional government which administered the unoccupied southern part of France. British, and Free French forces fighting on the Allied side, invaded Syria and Lebanon from Palestine in 1941, and quickly defeated the Vichy French troops.

There were already movements for Arab nationhood in the Middle East, some long established. The political uncertainty of the war meant that the ideas of Arab nationalism developed quickly. The Arabs wanted to govern themselves and saw their opportunity. There was a wave of hostility to Britain and France. That also produced some sympathy towards Nazi Germany and to Fascist Italy among some politically conscious Arabs.

The first Muslim fundamentalist movement had sprung up among Egyptian Sunni Muslims in 1928. This was the Muslim Brotherhood, founded by an Egyptian teacher and preacher, Hassan al-Banna. During the war, the Brotherhood took an anti-British line. Meanwhile, anti-British feeling became widespread in Egypt as the British army appeared to be facing defeat in the Western Desert. Egyptian politicians turned

The first day of the battle of El Alamein, 1942. After gaps had been cleared in enemy minefields, British tanks moved forward to join the fight.

against the Allies, until the Allies began to beat the Germans. Many Egyptian Army officers took an anti-British line including, by his own account, Anwar al-Sadat, who was to be President of Egypt from 1970 to 1981.

Elsewhere in the Arab world there were other nationalist and anti-Allied movements. In Syria, before the war, a new movement called the Ba'ath Party was founded by young intellectual Syrians who were educated in France. The most influential thinker of the Ba'ath Party was a Christian Arab political activist, Michel Aflaq.

The Ba'ath Party was the first Arab movement to begin to set out the ideas of Arab independence and self-determination, as well as the pan-Arab ideal that Arabs of different countries should have a single political movement. The movement taught that all Arabs should belong to one nation, and that the wealth of the Arab world should be used for the good of all the people.

In Palestine, Arab nationalists thought the war might help them to get rid of the British. An influential nationalist in Palestine was Hajj Amin al-Husseini – the Mufti of Jerusalem, a leading Sunni Muslim religious dignitary – who was also a member of one of Palestine's leading families. He disliked the British and engaged in discussions with the Germans and Italians, who issued a declaration in favour of Arab independence in 1940.

In Iraq, in 1941, the Iraqi politician Rashid Ali al-Kilani attempted, with German encouragement, to stage a revolt against the British while the British forces were occupied elsewhere. However, the British soon regained control.

Britain's last attempt to keep its position in the Middle East was a new international agreement known as the Baghdad Pact, signed in 1955. The members of the Pact were Britain, Iraq, Turkey, Iran and Pakistan. The USA was an associate member. The pact was meant to bind the Middle East states to the West, and to defend the Middle East and its oil against possible attacks from the Soviet Union, which had emerged as a superpower to rival the USA after the Second World War.

But the Pact failed. One reason was that Egypt's

Lieutenant-Colonel Nasser at the time he assumed the presidency of Egypt, 1954 (see page 16). He became a powerful Arab leader.

new leader, President Nasser, who was very influential, saw the Pact as just a way for the old colonialists to keep control of the Middle East. He refused to join the Pact, and in due course he looked to the Soviet Union for military and financial assistance.

Another Middle Eastern state which refused membership of the Pact was Jordan, which was also unable to join because of internal political opposition, some of it from supporters of Nasser. And in Iraq, after the first Iraqi military coup in 1958 when the monarchy fell, the new revolutionary regime withdrew.

After that the Pact, and with it the last remnants of the colonial relationship between the West and the Middle East, withered away. That was in effect the end of the colonial era in the Middle East. From then on, the USA and the Soviet Union became the principal outside influences.

CHAPTER 5

1948 AND ISRAEL

The foundation of the State of Israel was declared on 14 May 1948 by David Ben-Gurion and other Zionist leaders. It was perhaps the most important date in the recent story of the Middle East; millions of words have been written about the rights and wrongs of the establishment of Israel.

For Jews around the world Israel was seen as the salvation of a much persecuted people. In Europe, Hitler had slaughtered millions of Jews in a massacre now known as the Holocaust. Nevertheless, the Arabs believe that the Jews wrongfully took the Arab land of Palestine in 1948.

How did it happen that a Jewish state came into existence in the Arab Middle East? Of course, Palestine was the historic home of the Jews in ancient times, and it was the aim of people called Zionists to have a Jewish state there once again. The Zionists were Jews who wanted to return to the area from which Jewish people originated and to set up a Jewish state where they could be free of anti-semitism. Among their leaders were Chaim Weizmann, a British Jew of Russian origin, who was to become Israel's first president, and Polish-born David Ben-Gurion who had been in Palestine since he was a young man.

From the start of the British Mandate in 1920, up to 1936, the British authorities had honoured the promise implied in the Balfour Declaration by allowing the immigration of Jews into Palestine. The increasing persecution of Jews in Germany and elsewhere in Europe led to a growth in Jewish immigration. In 1936 the Palestinian Arabs began to protest, and fearing trouble the British cut the Jewish influx.

The declaration of the Independent State of Israel on 14 May 1948 was greeted with jubilation by its new citizens.

An Arab evacuee, one of thousands who left Jewish-held areas during the 1948 Arab–Israeli conflict, is interviewed by a Red Cross worker.

In Palestine, after the war, Jewish resistance organizations such as the Haganah and the Irgun fought a guerrilla war against the British. The most spectacular incident, in 1946, was the bombing of the King David Hotel, where the British Mandate offices were located. More than ninety people died in this attack. Politicians such as the former prime minister and leader of Israel's Likud Party, Yitzhak Shamir, were involved with these guerrilla organizations.

At the end of the Second World War, the Arab population of Palestine was over a million and the Jewish population about half a million, with more Jews trying to come from Europe. In August 1947, the United Nations (the international organization formed in 1945 to promote peace and security) recommended the partition of Palestine, but the Arabs refused to accept the plan. As war between Jews and Arabs began to look inevitable, many Arabs left their homes for the safety of neighbouring Arab countries.

In 1948, Britain terminated the Palestine Mandate and the State of Israel was declared immediately. Fighting between Jews and Arabs in Palestine had already begun, and afterwards the governments of the neighbouring Arab states became involved. The Arabs proclaimed their intention to destroy the Jewish state, but were in the event easily defeated. More Arabs left their homes during the war and became refugees.

In the armistice talks of 1949 between Israel and the Arabs, Israel claimed more territory than the original United Nations (UN) partition plan had promised the Jews. Meanwhile, most of the rest of Palestine came under Jordanian administration and was annexed in 1949 by Jordan, while a small area in the south-east on the Mediterranean coast, known as the Gaza Strip, was administered by Egypt. Israel was to keep its 1949 frontiers until the war of 1967, which we shall read about in Chapter 8 (page 20).

The Palestinian people refer to the events of 1948 as 'the catastrophe'. Though some Palestinians stayed in Israel, especially in the northern part of the country, and have become Arab citizens of Israel, many became refugees. Israel began as a Jewish state with the world's good wishes. But over the years sympathy for Israel has waned.

'There is probably no accounting for the mass exodus [of Palestinians] without understanding the prevalence and depth of the general sense of collapse, of "falling apart", that permeated Arab Palestine, especially the towns, by April 1948. With the offensives of the Haganah, the cumulative effect of the fears, deprivations, abandonment and depredations [plundering] of the previous months overcame the natural basic reluctance to abandon home and property and go into exile. Arab morale cracked, giving way to general and blind panic. The urban masses and the peasants, however, had nowhere to go, certainly not in comfort. For them, flight meant instant destitution.'
(Benny Morris, *Guardian Weekly*, 20 March 1988.)

CHAPTER 6

SUEZ AND NASSER

On 26 July 1956 President Gamal Abdel Nasser of Egypt precipitated a crisis in the Middle East when he nationalized the Suez Canal, which runs from the Mediterranean to the Red Sea and provides a vital route for sea traffic from Asia to Europe.

The Suez Canal had been previously owned by a European company based in Paris, in which Britain owned nearly half the shares. The Canal was seen as vital to world trade. Britain's Prime Minister Anthony Eden was determined to recover the Canal and to make Nasser back down.

British and French troops invaded the Suez Canal zone of Egypt in November 1956, with the assistance of forces from the young State of Israel. Israeli forces were sent by Prime Minister Ben-Gurion to occupy the Sinai Peninsula, where Israel had some strategic objectives. In retaliation, Egypt blocked the Canal by sinking the ships that were passing through it.

But in the end it was Britain and France that were humiliated. They were forced to withdraw by the USA, which used financial sanctions against them. Israel also pulled out of Sinai at the insistence of America. President Eisenhower had not been consulted before the troops moved in, and he was furious at the display of European aggression.

Egypt's strategy demonstrated that the era of British and French colonial power was effectively over. The Canal was reopened for navigation in April 1957, with Egyptian pilots and managers.

The seizure of the Suez Canal established Nasser's standing in the Arab world, and as a Third World leader. He had come to power in Egypt in 1952 at the age of 34, as the leader of a group of young officers who carried out a coup against what they saw as the corrupt old regime. The members of the group called themselves the Free Officers. The revolutionaries deposed Egypt's last king, King Farouk. Nasser himself took over as president in 1954.

US intervention brought the Suez crisis to an end, but the USA had also had a hand in causing it. Egypt's new rulers had wanted modern weapons, but the USA would not provide them. So, in 1955 Nasser made an agreement to buy arms from the Soviet Union, using Czechoslovakia as an intermediary.

An aerial view of the Suez Canal during the crisis of 1956, showing the ships sunk by Egypt to block the canal.

The US Secretary of State, John Foster Dulles, retaliated to this so-called 'Czech arms deal' in 1956. He cut off aid promised to Egypt to build a huge dam on the Nile in Upper Egypt. Without US aid, Nasser said he needed the revenue from the Canal to provide Egypt with its own funds to build the Aswan High Dam.

The dam was eventually built with Soviet help and today still supplies Egypt with much of its electric power. The Soviet leader, Nikita Khrushchev, attended the opening ceremony in 1964.

The Aswan High Dam, built by Egypt on the upper reaches of the River Nile, created a new resource for fishing, leisure, tourism, and hydroelectric power.

CHAPTER 7

OPEC AND OIL

The Middle East contains two-thirds of the world's oil. Today oil is the world's principal source of energy and is likely to remain so for the rest of the century and well into the next millennium. A quarter of the world's oil is in Saudi Arabia alone, eight times more than in the USA, which is the world's largest oil consumer.

OPEC, the Organization of Petroleum Exporting Countries, was set up at an inaugural meeting which took place in the Iraqi capital, Baghdad, in September 1960. The oil exporting countries were determined to take control of their own resources, and most of all, to control oil prices. Today, OPEC has thirteen members, in the Middle East and Africa as well as Latin America and South East Asia.

The aims of the Arab oil producers were initially economic rather than political. The only political issue on which all the Arab oil producers could unite was the Palestinian problem. The Arab countries first made the attempt to wield what became known as 'the oil weapon' – that is, the threat to withhold oil supplies from the

The most efficient way of transporting oil from its point of production is by massive pipelines. Once it reaches the coast it is piped on to vast oil tankers for export to countries all over the world.

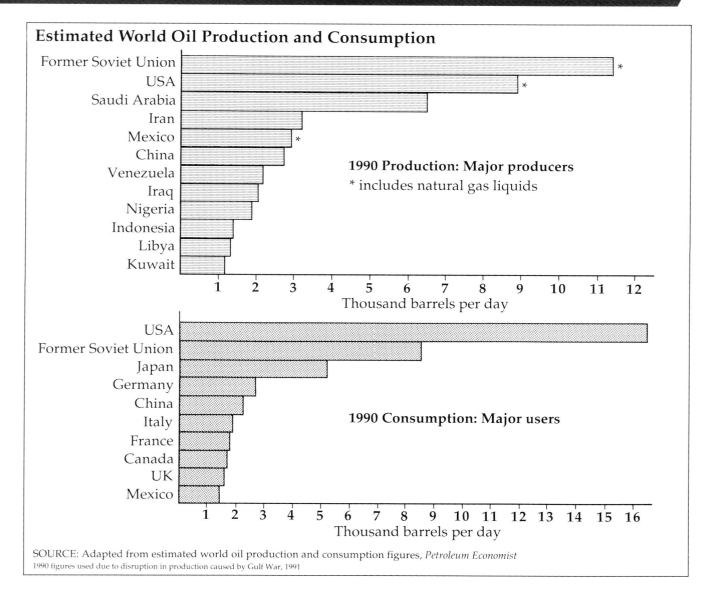

Estimated World Oil Production and Consumption

1990 Production: Major producers
* includes natural gas liquids

Thousand barrels per day

1990 Consumption: Major users

Thousand barrels per day

SOURCE: Adapted from estimated world oil production and consumption figures, *Petroleum Economist*
1990 figures used due to disruption in production caused by Gulf War, 1991

West, or to increase prices in a punitive way – after the Arab–Israeli War of 1967 (see next chapter).

In 1968 the Arab states improved their ability to act together politically when they formed OAPEC, the Organization of Arab Petroleum Exporting Countries. The Arab countries also remained members of OPEC.

In 1973, after the next Arab–Israeli War (see Chapter 11, page 26) the OPEC and OAPEC countries were able to impose a price rise along with cutbacks in supply. This enabled the oil-producing countries to impose sanctions on the economies of the oil-consuming states, in order to get a favourable post-war settlement for the Arabs, without suffering shortfalls of income. Since then OPEC has been a major factor in the oil market.

But in the 1980s, though OPEC reserves remained high, OPEC production fell to only a third of the world's total because of discoveries and exploitation elsewhere, in Africa, Europe and the Americas. That meant OPEC could no longer dictate world oil prices. In 1986 oil prices fell to their lowest point in recent times.

OPEC tries to maximize the revenues of its members. But it can only do so by attempting to keep production low in order to drive up the market price. OPEC has limited control over oil prices today.

CHAPTER 8

THE ARAB–ISRAELI WAR OF 1967

The June War between Israel and the Arabs lasted just six days. It resulted in a sweeping military victory for the Israelis. Israel captured territory from Egypt, Jordan and Syria. When the war was over, Israeli leaders spoke of their relief that Israel had survived.

The war began on 5 June 1967, when Israel's air force launched a devastating series of attacks on Egyptian airfields which destroyed most of Egypt's aircraft on the ground. Technically, Israel was the aggressor, since Israel fired the first shots.

But before the war broke out, Egypt had been aggressive. In May 1967 President Nasser ordered UN troops out of Sinai, and he blockaded the Strait of Tiran, Israel's only access to its one southern seaport of Eilat. Egypt signed a military pact with Syria in May 1967. On 30 May, King Hussein of Jordan joined that pact, and on 4 June Iraq followed suit.

Egypt's version of events on the other hand, is that Egyptian diplomats around the world were trying to calm the situation and slow down what seemed to be a progression towards war when Israel struck.

Rapid mobilization of troops and vehicles in the desert allowed Israel to greatly increase its territory in only six days of war.

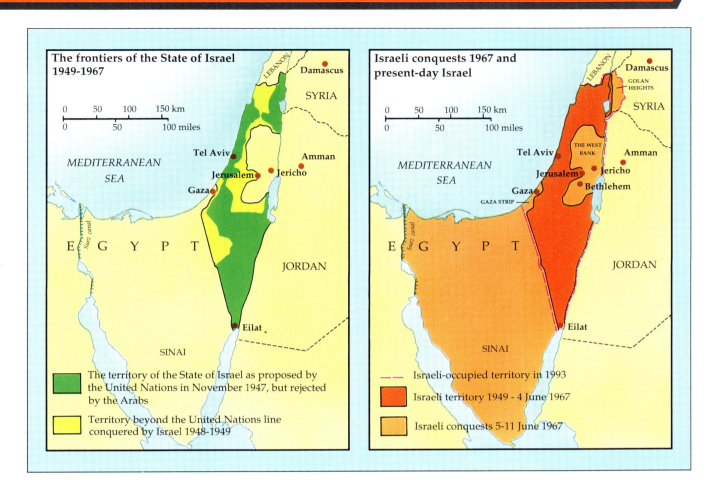

The frontiers of the State of Israel 1949-1967

0 50 100 150 km
0 50 100 miles

MEDITERRANEAN SEA

LEBANON
Damascus
SYRIA
Tel Aviv
Amman
Jerusalem Jericho
Gaza
EGYPT
JORDAN
Eilat
SINAI

■ The territory of the State of Israel as proposed by the United Nations in November 1947, but rejected by the Arabs

■ Territory beyond the United Nations line conquered by Israel 1948-1949

Israeli conquests 1967 and present-day Israel

0 50 100 150 km
0 50 100 miles

MEDITERRANEAN SEA

LEBANON
Damascus
GOLAN HEIGHTS
SYRIA
Tel Aviv
THE WEST BANK
Amman
Jerusalem Jericho
Gaza Bethlehem
GAZA STRIP
EGYPT
JORDAN
Eilat
SINAI

– – – Israeli-occupied territory in 1993

■ Israeli territory 1949 - 4 June 1967

■ Israeli conquests 5-11 June 1967

Israel's territory before and after the 1967 war.

In the event the war was disastrous for Egypt and for the Arabs. On 6 and 7 June the Israelis quickly overran the whole of Sinai as they had in 1956. On 7 June Jordan lost the Old City of Jerusalem and the West Bank, and on 9 June Syria lost a strip of territory in the Golan Heights, which overlooks Galilee in northern Israel. The fighting ended on 10 June.

For the Arabs, and particularly for President Nasser of Egypt, the war brought despair. Nasser offered his resignation to the Egyptian people, but they begged him to stay. Nasser held himself personally responsible for Egypt's military collapse.

On 22 November 1967, the UN Security Council unanimously passed its Resolution 242, calling for Israel to withdraw from the territories it had occupied and to make peace with the Arabs on the basis of its pre-1967 frontiers.

But Israel did not withdraw. Many countries and international organizations still regard Resolution 242 as an essential part of any future settlement between the Arabs and Israel.

After the end of the June War, border tension continued between Egypt and Israel. In the next three years, a thousand Israelis and many times that number of Egyptians lost their lives in border incidents. This was known as the 'war of attrition'. The Israelis built a fortified line, known as the Bar Lev, along the eastern bank of the Suez Canal.

President Nasser never recovered personally or politically from the defeat. He collapsed suddenly while trying to reconcile the Palestinian factions and King Hussein of Jordan in 1970. Exhausted by stress, President Nasser died of a heart attack at his home in Cairo on 28 September 1970.

CHAPTER 9

THE LIBYAN REVOLUTION AND COLONEL GADDAFI

On 1 September 1969 the former Kingdom of Libya awoke to discover it had a new ruler, a young army officer, Captain Muammar Gaddafi. The military coup organized by Colonel Gaddafi, as he now is, came without warning. Even in Libya's neighbour, Egypt, nobody knew at first what the aims of the new rulers were.

Before the Second World War, Libya had been an Italian colony, and after the war it was run by a British and French military administration. Libya became independent in 1951 as a monarchy ruled by King Idris, formerly the hereditary ruler of the eastern part of the country known as Cyrenaica.

Libya was a poor country until oil was discovered there in the 1950s. The belief of oil geologists that Libya was a potential oil-producing country was justified, and oil income rose from a very modest beginning of $3 million in 1961 to over $1 billion ten years later.

Under King Idris, the US oil companies played a large part in Libya's affairs, while the USA also maintained a large air base at Wheelus Field, near Tripoli. With a pro-Western King, Libya seemed set to settle into the same conservative pattern as the oil states of the Gulf.

Gaddafi put a stop to all that. He immediately declared himself to be a fervent supporter of Egypt's Colonel Nasser, and put himself firmly in the Arab revolutionary camp. This did not stop him from making a major arms deal with France in the 1970s. Since then, his relations with his neighbours have fluctuated. After some quarrels, he was on better terms with Egypt by

A rare view of Colonel Gaddafi in civilian clothes (left) as he leaves a mosque with President Assad of Syria (centre) and Egypt's President Sadat (Nasser's successor). The photograph was taken during a meeting between the three Arab leaders in 1971.

1992, and Libya continued to be a member of the Arab Maghreb Union, which links it with Algeria, Tunisia, Morocco and Mauritania.

But though the West wanted to continue exploiting Libya's oil, the Western countries have found it hard to approve of Gaddafi. The USA, in particular, has become convinced that Gaddafi's support for terrorist movements is a danger. The extremist Palestinian movement, usually known as the Abu Nidal faction, has based itself in Libya.

The former US President, Ronald Reagan, was violently opposed to Colonel Gaddafi. Reagan was angered in 1985 by the hijack of the *Achille Lauro*, a Mediterranean cruise ship, with the death of a US passenger. US planes eventually attacked Tripoli in April 1986 in retaliation for Libya's alleged involvement in the deaths of US servicemen in a terrorist bombing at a discotheque in Germany. But in the Arab world, the US attack aroused sympathy for Gaddafi, who previously had been widely distrusted.

In 1992, the UN imposed sanctions on Libya to obtain the extradition of two Libyans suspected of planting the bomb which destroyed a US passenger aircraft in 1988 (see box). The US government wanted to have the two suspects tried before a court outside Libya.

On 21 December 1988, Pan Am flight 103 from London to New York exploded over the small town of Lockerbie in Scotland. All 258 people on board the plane were killed, plus about twenty people in Lockerbie itself. More than forty homes were destroyed.

An eyewitness reported that 'the scene was like "hell on earth", with buildings on fire and people running in the streets screaming'. Investigations revealed that a bomb on board the plane had caused the explosion, and the Palestinian terrorist group Abu Nidal, based in Libya, was suspected of planting it.

A great gouge of earth and wrecked houses in the village of Lockerbie show the path of the crashing plane.

CHAPTER 10

TERRORISM AND THE PLO

In 1970, some Palestinian factions decided that only spectacular terrorist acts, which would capture the world's attention, would make sure that the Palestinian cause was not forgotten. On 6 September 1970, Palestinian guerrillas of the PFLP, a small extremist Palestinian faction, hijacked two jet airliners, one US and the other Swiss, and brought them to a remote desert airstrip in Jordan called Dawson's Field. Other hijacks included a failed attempt on an Israeli jet bound for New York, when the hijackers were overcome by Israeli security men. A few days later a third airliner, this time British, was brought to the same airstrip.

PLO Chairman, Yasser Arafat, (right) greets President Rafsanjani of Iran at an Islamic summit meeting.

One of the terrorists from the Israeli plane was Leila Khaled who was held in London, and it was partly to bargain for her release that the British plane was taken. To Israel's anger, Leila Khaled was later allowed to go free. After days of tense negotiation, the passengers were released and the planes were blown up.

The Palestinian Liberation Organization, or PLO, is the body which includes all the Palestinian guerrilla groups. The PLO Chairman, Yasser Arafat, is himself the leader of Fatah, the largest Palestinian guerrilla organization. He did not approve of the hijackings. There were strong disagreements about action and on ideology between Arafat and more radical leaders such as the PFLP's George Habash.

Arafat became Chairman of the PLO in 1969. The PLO's aim was to liberate Palestinian territory from Israel. This meant the whole territory of Israel, since the Palestinians did not accept the legitimacy of the State of Israel.

After the war of 1967, the Palestinian guerrillas from the West Bank crossed the Jordan River with thousands of other refugees into Jordan proper. Law and order began to break down and the authority of King Hussein was challenged. To the Palestinians it was more important to prepare themselves for the confrontation with Israel than to obey King Hussein.

King Hussein decided to fight back in order to uphold his authority. On 17 September 1970 the Jordanian army tackled the guerrillas. In the battle between the king's army and the guerrillas the Jordanian forces won. This episode provided a name for a new and more radical PFLP group which called itself Black September.

This group went on to commit more terrorist acts. They assassinated the Jordanian prime minister in Cairo in 1971, and killed eleven Israeli athletes at the Munich Olympic games in 1972. These and other terrorist incidents convinced the world, wrongly, that the Palestinian liberation movement was purely a terrorist organization.

In the 1980s, the PLO said its attitude had changed. Chairman Yasser Arafat announced his recognition of Israel and renunciation of violence at a special UN session in Geneva

Youths march during a PFLP rally. Their T-shirts bear the portrait of Omar Qassem, a PLO activist imprisoned for over 21 years and likened by the PLO to Nelson Mandela in South Africa.

in December 1988.

But the Palestinian movement still contains groups which have not renounced violence and reject all compromise over Palestine. These include the PFLP-General Command, and the Abu Nidal faction, supported by Iraq and Libya. Such groups continue to plan violent acts, partly to frustrate any efforts to negotiate for peace.

It can be asked why the PLO does not repudiate its connection with all who still believe in violence. The answer seems to be that Yasser Arafat believes that the PLO has a political destiny in Palestine, and that there should be no separate Palestinian groups which could challenge the PLO's claim to be the sole legitimate representative of the Palestinian people. If he tried to expel violent groups from the PLO, they might challenge the PLO's claim to be representative.

Palestinian groups and their leaders

Palestine Liberation Organization: the umbrella organization which contains all the Palestinian guerrilla groups, and reports to the Palestine National Council. The Chairman of the PLO is Yasser Arafat. The PLO's 'cabinet' is the fourteen-member Executive Committee.

Individual guerrilla groups are:

Fatah: the largest Palestinian group, whose leader is Yasser Arafat.

Popular Front for the Liberation of Palestine (PFLP): leader George Habash. More militant than Fatah, carries out attacks on Israel.

Democratic Front for the Liberation of Palestine (DFLP): leader Naif Hawatmeh. Also more militant; attacks on Israel.

PFLP-General Command: leader Ahmed Jibril. Terrorist acts.

Palestine Liberation Front (PLF): leader Abu'l Abbas. Terrorist acts.

Saiqa: controlled by Syria. Attacks on Israel.

Abu Nidal faction (sometimes known as Fatah Revolutionary Council): splinter group led by Abu Nidal. Terrorist acts.

CHAPTER 11

SADAT AND THE OCTOBER WAR

On 6 October 1973, Egyptian forces crossed the Suez Canal into Israeli-held Egyptian territory. Egypt's revenge for the defeat of 1967 had begun. Though the October War ended in no clear victory for either side, Egypt inflicted some defeats on the Israeli forces. The war began the diplomatic process which led to Egypt's recovery of Sinai, and in the longer run to Egypt's peace treaty with Israel.

It was Egypt's President Anwar Sadat who decided the time had come for Egypt to go on the offensive. Sadat succeeded to the presidency after Nasser's death in 1970. He had been a member of the original revolutionary group of Free Officers, and one of Nasser's vice-presidents. By 1971, Sadat was firmly in control.

In July 1972 Sadat told the USSR that all the Soviet military advisers in Egypt brought in by Nasser had to leave. Sadat believed that the Soviets had decided to try to stop Egypt from fighting. Without their restraining hand, Sadat planned and carried out his attack on Israel.

In two weeks of war the Egyptians held their positions on the east bank of the Suez Canal, but the Israelis counter-attacked and crossed the Canal farther south, holding positions inside Egypt on the Canal's west bank. (See maps, page 21.) In the eventual cease-fire, Israel withdrew and took up positions some thirty kilometres east of the Canal.

In the aftermath of the war, Sadat was able to re-establish good relations with the USA. This began the increasingly warm relationship between Egypt and the USA which has lasted until the 1990s. In Israel, Prime Minister Golda Meir resigned, and Yitzhak Rabin became Prime Minister.

The USA's diplomacy during the 1970s resulted in disengagement agreements between Egypt and Israel. But the breakthrough in relations between Egypt and Israel came in November 1977 when President Sadat decided to travel to Israel himself to talk about the need for peace between the two countries.

After the first meeting between Sadat and the next Israeli prime minister, Menachem Begin, diplomacy moved rapidly under US guidance.

An elated Egyptian soldier in October 1973, soon after crossing the Suez Canal into Sinai, Egyptian territory which the Israelis had held since 1967. Behind him is one of the Egyptian pontoon bridges used to cross the Canal.

Friendliness which would have been unthinkable only a few years earlier: Israel's Prime Minister Begin (left) and President Sadat of Egypt at Camp David in America in 1978.

The agreements known as the Camp David Accords were signed by the two countries at the US president's country home in 1978. A peace treaty between Egypt and Israel followed in March 1979.

The other Arab states regarded this move as treachery to the Arab cause, and it was not until a decade later, long after Sadat's death, that Egypt was really accepted back into Arab diplomatic circles. In 1989, Egypt was readmitted to the Arab League, the international organization of Arab states.

Sadat was assassinated because Muslim fundamentalist groups detested both his peace treaty with Israel and the changes in Egyptian society brought about by closer contacts with the West. On 6 October 1981, on the eighth anniversary of the historic crossing of the Suez Canal by Egyptian troops, President Anwar Sadat was shot dead during a celebratory parade in Cairo by a small Muslim fundamentalist group which had infiltrated the army. But Sadat's vice-president, Hosni Mubarak, survived, and immediately became Egypt's new leader.

Henry Kissinger, former US Secretary of State, on the October War:
'Until then I had not taken Sadat seriously. Because of the many threats to go to war that had not been implemented I had dismissed him as more actor than statesman. Now I was beginning to understand that the grandiloquent [exaggerated] gestures were part of a conscious strategy. They had guaranteed surprise. The expulsion of the Soviet advisers from Egypt in 1972 suddenly took on a new significance. Sadat was right; if the Soviet advisers were to depart it had to be done all at once. Sadat wanted to be rid of the Soviets in order to remove an encumbrance both to the war he was planning, and to his projected move towards the United States.'
(Henry Kissinger, *Years of Upheaval*, 1982 .)

CHAPTER 12

LEBANON'S CIVIL WAR

On the fateful day of 13 April 1975, Lebanese Christian Phalangist militiamen ambushed a bus in the Beirut suburb of Ain el-Roumaneh, killing twenty-seven Palestinians. At the time, this seemed like an incident which was not too far out of the ordinary in a city which was home to various polarized and violent groups. In retrospect, it was the incident that sparked the Lebanese civil war.

The war, which lasted for over fifteen years, was an intensely complex struggle, involving militias from Lebanon's different Muslim and Christian populations, fighting for their own interests in a country in which different communities had previously lived together, if precariously. The Palestinians were also involved, and both Syria and Israel sent troops into Lebanon at different times.

In the end the factional struggles became so complex and fruitless that almost all Lebanese began to be willing to sacrifice their own interests to achieve peace, which by 1991 seemed to be within the government's grasp. By 1992 Lebanon was already considering plans to rebuild its war-shattered capital Beirut, which hopefully were not premature.

In 1975, the Muslim and Christian communities were closely balanced in numbers, with perhaps slightly more Muslims than Christians. The Shi'ites were the majority Muslim group, with 30 per cent of the population, while the Sunni Muslims had 20 per cent. In addition there were the Druzes, a sect whose religion differs from Islam but derives from it.

Lebanese communities Population (estimated): 3 million	
Shi'ite Muslim	35 per cent
Sunni Muslim	20 per cent
Druze	7 per cent
Maronite Christian	22 per cent
Other Christian	16 per cent
(includes Greek Orthodox, Orthodox, Catholic, Presbyterian and small sects)	

But the Christians, and to a lesser extent the Sunni Muslims, held power in Lebanon because of an agreement that the president was always to be a Maronite Christian, and the prime minister was always to be a Sunni Muslim.

The reason for the outbreak of civil war in 1975 was that the Sunni and Shi'ite Muslims in Lebanon, together with the Druzes and the Palestinians, began to resent the Christian domination of the country. After a year of war, in 1976, Syrian forces moved into Lebanon to try to restore stability, while Israel began to interfere across the southern Lebanese border. In 1978 UN troops moved into south Lebanon.

In June 1982, in a major military action ostensibly aimed at the defence of northern Israel, Israeli forces again moved into Lebanon. This time they pressed on as far as the suburbs of Beirut. The aim of Israel's minister of defence, Ariel Sharon, was to drive the PLO forces out of Lebanon and get a pro-Israeli government installed.

After the Palestinian fighters had left their positions and dispersed, hundreds of Palestinian civilians were massacred by Phalangist Christian militia controlled by the Gemayel family in notorious massacres at the refugee camps at Sabra and Shatila. The head of the Gemayel clan, Beshir Gemayel, was elected president in a move acceptable to the Israelis, but was almost immediately assassinated. In September 1982 his brother Amin Gemayel was elected in his place.

In 1983, the Israeli troops began to withdraw. Later in 1983, in the largest single terrorist attack during the war, nearly 241 US marines, who were in Lebanon as part of a multinational peace-keeping force, were killed in a single suicide bomb attack on their barracks.

In 1985, the PLO began to return to southern Lebanon. Also, with the encouragement of Islamic Iran, Shi'ite factions, including the militant, Iran-linked Hizbollah, began to emerge. Soon after this, the first Western hostages were taken. The aims of the hostage-takers were, for the most part, not clearly expressed and it was not clear what advantage they hoped to gain. Some eighty Western hostages in all were taken, of whom the last were released in June 1992.

At the end of Amin Gemayel's term as president in 1988, Lebanon was left without a head of state. The existing government claimed it was still legitimate. However the army commander-in-chief, General Aoun, also claimed he headed a legitimate government. There was a constitutional crisis, with two governments both claiming they were legitimate. There was also a

battle to drive Aoun out. He held out in East Beirut until the Syrian and Lebanese armies drove him into exile in 1990.

The problems of Lebanon seemed insoluble, but in the end, Arab diplomacy broke the deadlock. Saudi Arabia invited the remaining members of Lebanon's National Assembly to a meeting at Taif in Saudi Arabia in September 1989, to discuss Lebanon's future. The Taif agreement has opened the way for real power-sharing between the communities. It also called for the dissolution of the militias.

By 1992 major problems continued only in south Lebanon, where armed Hizbollah fighters confronted Israel and the South Lebanon Army. However, on the whole, Lebanon seemed to be relatively calm.

Houses in the Lebanese capital, Beirut, devastated and raked by gunfire; legacy of more than fifteen years of civil war.

CHAPTER 13

ISLAMIC IRAN

Until 1979, Iran had been governed by the Shah. But Ayatollah Khomeini (see box) returned to Tehran on 1 February 1979 after fifteen years of exile. His return was a remarkable event. There have been estimates that up to 3 million people came out to welcome him as he drove into Tehran from the airport.

Khomeini's return followed the collapse of the government of the Shah. The Shah had been pro-Western and had tried to modernize Iran, but he had ignored both democracy and his people's right to civil liberty. The Shah inherited the throne from his father (who had to abdicate in 1941, when Iran was under threat from the Soviet Union and from internal communist revolution) and had became increasingly autocratic during his reign.

Khomeini had immense public support and soon drove out the interim government the Shah had left behind. Khomeini's first act was to draft an Islamic constitution. Fundamentalist Muslims believe there should be no distinction between religion and politics. A Muslim state should be governed according to Islam. But in practice, rules needed to be worked out in what was the world's first fully Islamic state since the days of Muhammad himself. Iran is the home of the Shi'ite branch of Islam, which is especially receptive to the idea of an Islamic state.

The Shah of Iran and his wife, shown in 1967. The Shah lived a privileged, Western lifestyle and his increasingly harsh treatment of political opponents eventually proved his downfall.

By December 1979, a new Islamic constitution was approved by a referendum, giving Iran an elected president, and an elected assembly, but also giving power to the Faqi, a spiritual leader, a position to be held by Khomeini himself. Khomeini also became head of the armed forces, and set up the Revolutionary Guards, a paramilitary body alongside the regular army and police.

In November 1979, militants had already seized the US Embassy in Tehran, in a gesture which showed the new Islamic Republic's hostility to the USA and also its disregard for international diplomatic conventions. The fifty-two members of the Embassy staff taken hostage were held until January 1981.

In spite of the beginning of the war between Iraq and Iran in September 1980 (see Chapter 15, page 34), Iran's Islamic Republic continued with its self-imposed task of transforming Iranian

Ayatollah Khomeini (with the white beard to the left) was greeted by massive, enthusiastic crowds on his triumphant return to Iran in 1979.

society according to an Islamic model, and with developing its new political institutions.

Khomeini died in June 1989, and the scenes of hysteria and grief from the immense crowd at his funeral amazed television audiences worldwide. He was succeeded as Faqi by Hojatolislam Ali Khameini, who had been president while Khomeini lived. Hojatolislam Ali Akbar Rafsanjani was elected president in July 1989.

Under the new regime, effective power has passed from the Faqi, the spiritual leader, to President Rafsanjani. By 1992 Iran was concerning itself with its political position in the Gulf, with its role as a world Islamic power, and with putting its relations with Western and other countries back on to a normal footing after the upheavals of the 1980s.

'Sayyid Ruhallah Musavi Khomeini was the son of Sayyid Mustafa Musavi, the chief cleric of Khomein, a town 350 kilometres from Tehran. His father was murdered when he was a year old . . . In 1925 he completed his studies in Muslim law, ethics and spiritual philosophy . . . Over the years he established himself as a teacher who related ethical and spiritual problems to contemporary social issues. In 1941 he attacked secularism and Reza Pahlavi Shah's dictatorial rule . . . In 1961 he became an Ayatollah [the highest religious post]. In 1963 he vehemently attacked the Shah and his secular pro-Western policies. This speech transformed him into a national hero among the religious masses. In 1964 he was deported to Turkey, and then kept up his campaign from the Shi'ite shrine at Najaf in Iraq. Khomeini was a pious principled man of strong convictions, extremely patient and shrewd, fearless and uncompromising. He led a spartan life and was incorruptible. All these qualities gave him a charisma which no other Iranian leader, religious or secular, had so far enjoyed. He deplored Arab nationalism, which he saw, he said in a newspaper interview, "as fundamentally opposed to Islam and its desire to abolish nationality and unite all mankind in a single community, indifferent to the matter of race and colour". On February 1st [1979] he returned to Tehran in triumph from France, where he had been living in exile.'
(Abridged from *The Longest War*, Dilip Hiro, 1989.)

CHAPTER 14

SADDAM HUSSEIN AND HAFEZ AL-ASSAD

S addam Hussein of Iraq and President Assad of Syria have much in common. Both head Ba'athist governments and are strong, ruthless rulers.

Saddam Hussein of Iraq

In July 1979, President Saddam Hussein was formally sworn in as President of the Republic of Iraq. Previously deputy leader of the government, he had for some time been viewed as Iraq's most important decision maker.

Saddam Hussein was born in 1937 in the town of Takrit, north of Baghdad. He is a Sunni Muslim. He joined the Ba'ath Party in 1957, when it was illegal in Iraq. In 1959, he took part in an attempted coup against the Iraqi ruler, General Kassem, and when it failed, fled the country. He returned to Iraq from Egypt in 1963 after Kassem's overthrow, and began his ascent of the Ba'ath's ladder of power.

The Iraqi leader has always had a reputation for ruthlessness. He has never shrunk from action against any individual or group which offended him or stood in his way. That has included action against Iraq's Shi'ite and Kurdish populations. More than half of Iraq's population of 18 million is Shi'ite, and lives in the south of the country where the most important Shi'ite shrines are located. Up to 4 million Kurds live in the north of the country.

Two armed girls, members of Saddam Hussein's youth movement, pose with their friends in front of a portrait of the Iraqi president.

Saddam Hussein has been responsible for much conflict in the Middle East. In 1980, he started the war between Iran and Iraq, which plunged the country into ten years of hardship and sacrifice (see Chapter 15, page 34); and in 1990 he launched the Gulf War when his troops invaded Kuwait (Chapter 17, page 38).

Saddam Hussein's Ba'athist regime is, in theory, based on the ideas of Arab unity and social justice. In practice Iraq's government is authoritarian and pragmatic.

Hafez al-Assad of Syria

The regime in Syria is also Ba'athist, though Syria's President Hafez al-Assad is a bitter enemy of Saddam Hussein and the two regimes are irreconcilably opposed. President Assad came to power in a coup in 1970 and, like Hussein in

Iraq, eliminated his opponents in Syria in a ruthless manner. Assad faced his biggest challenge in 1980 when Muslim Brotherhood members and others organized protests. Dissent was strong in Syria's northern cities and culminated in a massive army attack on Hama in 1982.

Just as Saddam Hussein has put members of his own family into key positions and gave jobs to people from his home town of Takrit, Assad has relied on members of the sect of Islam to which he belongs, the Alawi. This is a minority group with specific religious beliefs from the north-west of Syria.

Staying in power

Though in practice they are dictators, President Assad of Syria and President Saddam Hussein of Iraq are not without their supporters. In each country, many people know their own position depends on the continuation of the current regime. But in each case, the strength of

the regimes is of a personal nature, and the death or deposition of either leader would bring upheaval.

A former hostage in Lebanon, American Terry Anderson (centre), greets the world's press after being released into the care of the Syrian government, in 1991. A photo of Syria's President Assad hangs on the wall above. In helping with the release of Western hostages, President Assad gained considerable prestige with Western governments.

CHAPTER 15

THE IRAN–IRAQ WAR

President Saddam Hussein gave the order for Iraq's attack on Iran to begin on 22 September 1980. His aim was to take control of the waterway lying between the two countries, the Shatt al-Arab. He also wanted, if he could, to annex territory in the south-west of Iran, which contains a minority population of Arabic speakers. He also hoped to topple Iran's new Shi'ite revolutionary regime, which he feared might incite Iraq's own Shi'ite population to revolt against him.

At first, Iran was still disorganized after the Islamic Revolution of the previous year, and the Iraqi forces made rapid gains. However, Iraq underestimated Iran's ability to organize itself quickly. Iraq was never able to press far into Iran's territory, and by 1982, Iran was able to counter-attack.

In 1983, Iran carried its counter-attack into Iraq. Huge forces of Iranian troops were beaten back, with difficulty, by Iraq's artillery and airpower, and it began to emerge that Iraq was using chemical weapons such as mustard gas, a poison gas first used in Europe in the First World War (see box, page 41). Iran's young recruits died in large numbers on the war's appalling battlefields.

Iraq then began its air attacks against Iran's oil installations, and in the Gulf, Iran sank oil-tankers which were trading with Iraq. Iran even threatened to close the Gulf to shipping. These attacks on oil supplies drew in the Western powers, which mounted naval patrols to protect shipping in the Gulf. The two countries also began to attack each other's cities with missiles.

May 1984: members of Iran's Islamic Revolutionary Guard march to demonstrate support for their government's battle with Iraq.

(Left) Iraqi soldiers on the front line of the Iran–Iraq war, near Basra, show their loyalty to Saddam Hussein's leadership.

(Below) A wounded Iraqi child and his mother, victims of an air strike. Many children suffered appalling injuries because they went on to the roof tops to watch the war in the air – unaware that this was the most vulnerable place to be.

In January 1987, Iran launched an attack at the Iraqi city of Basra, which looked at first as if it might succeed and certainly alarmed the Iraqi regime. Iran's stated war aims included huge reparations and the removal of Saddam Hussein. Many people in Iraq believed Iran might now win the war.

But Iran's attack failed, and stalemate ensued. Meanwhile, at sea there were dangerous developments. For example, in May 1987 Iraq attacked a US Navy ship with an Exocet missile, killing 37 crew members. In July 1988, the USA shot down over the Gulf an Iranian civilian airliner killing 290 people.

In July 1987, the UN Security Council adopted its Resolution 598, calling for a cease-fire and the opening of peace negotiations. A year later, in July 1988, both sides accepted a cease-fire. No territory was gained by either side, and in 1990 Iraq signed an agreement with Iran restoring the pre-war agreement over the Shatt al-Arab.

The war was enormously costly for both countries and the casualties were vast. Yet little was changed by it. The question of the border between the two countries, access to the Red Sea, the control of the Gulf, and the ultimate issue of

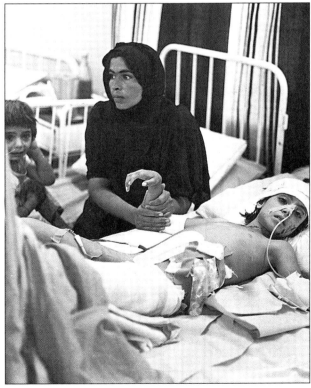

the control of oil resources remain in the long run unresolved, and antagonism between Iran and Iraq could resurface in the wake of the 1991 Gulf War.

CHAPTER 16

THE INTIFADA

The Palestinian uprising, or *intifada*, began on 8 December 1987. The troubles started when an Israeli truck crashed into Palestinian vehicles, apparently deliberately, killing four residents of Jabaliya refugee camp. Over the next few days, disturbances spread throughout Gaza and to towns and refugee camps in the West Bank, as well as in Jerusalem itself. Crowds of Palestinian demonstrators throwing stones and occasional Molotov cocktails, and building barriers with burning tyres, were confronted by Israeli troops with tear gas, water cannons and guns.

Gaza is a small area left unoccupied by Israel in the war of 1948, which filled up with Arab refugees from elsewhere in Palestine. It was administered by Egypt until the 1967 conflict. (See maps, pages 20–1.)

Only 45 kilometres long and 8 kilometres wide, it has a population of half a million, half of them refugees crammed into camps with primitive accommodation. Meanwhile some 850,000 Palestinians live in the occupied West Bank, and another 150,000 live in East Jerusalem, which the Israelis regard as part of Israel proper.

The *intifada* became a sustained and deliberate campaign against the continued Israeli occupation of the Palestinian lands taken by Israel in the war of 1967. As early as January

Israeli troops in front of a Palestinian refugee camp in the Israeli-occupied area of the Gaza strip. Many people have lived in camps such as these, in extreme poverty and squalid housing, since the Arab–Israeli war of 1948.

1988, leaflets announcing the formation of the Unified National Command of the *intifada* appeared throughout the Occupied Territories.

Unfortunately, the Palestinians have themselves begun to forfeit some sympathy. This is because many Palestinians have been suspected, often on very flimsy grounds, of being collaborators and have been killed by other Palestinians. In the *intifada*'s first four years, 470 Palestinians were killed this way while 850 were killed by the Israeli security forces.

Some problems within the Palestinian movement have come from the split between the Unified Command and an Islamic group which has called itself *Hamas*. There is a rift in the Palestinian movement between those who see

The greatest success of the *intifada* has come from its tactics. The Palestinians have mainly limited themselves to stone-throwing and demonstrations, and the protests have been carried out mostly by young people. There has been little in the way of armed attacks on Israelis. But Israel's response has been heavy-handed and violent. The spectacle shown on the world's television screens of armed Israeli troops shooting at and beating unarmed Palestinians, sometimes mere children, has cost Israel much international sympathy.

the struggle as an Islamic one, and those who are simply fighting for their liberty.

The Palestinian negotiators at the Middle East Peace Talks who represent the Palestinians of the Occupied Territories, have stressed that they do not believe the talks would have been held if it had not been for the years of popular uprising.

CHAPTER 17

THE GULF WAR

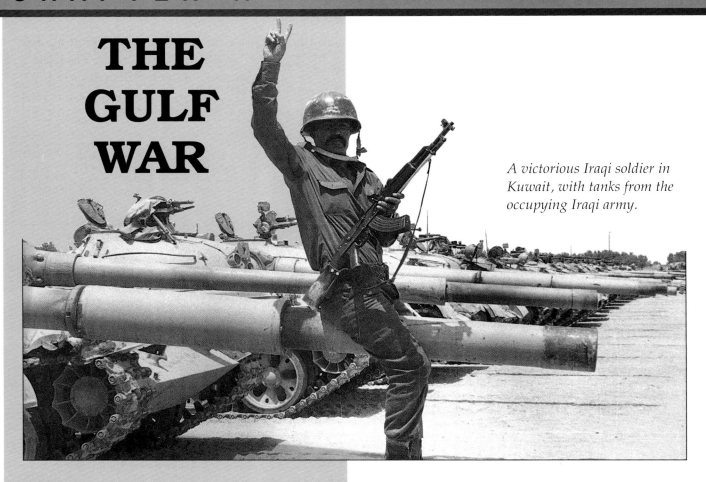

A victorious Iraqi soldier in Kuwait, with tanks from the occupying Iraqi army.

On 2 August 1990, President Saddam Hussein of Iraq sent his troops to invade Kuwait, beginning the Gulf crisis and the Gulf War. The Gulf crisis held the attention of the world until the Allied troops drove Iraq's forces out of Kuwait in February and March of 1991.

Iraq had grievances against Kuwait. For many years, Iraq had claimed part, or even all, of Kuwait's territory, and Iraq coveted Kuwait's oil-producing capacity. But though some kind of Iraqi action to annex part of northern Kuwait had seemed possible, nobody expected Saddam Hussein to send in his army and seize the whole country. The world was stunned. For one state to attempt to annex the whole of another seemed almost unthinkable.

The UN and the countries of the West condemned Iraq's action and demanded that its forces should leave Kuwait. On 2 August, only hours after the invasion, the UN Security Council passed its Resolution 660 calling for Iraq to withdraw its troops. But Iraq declared the annexation of Kuwait, which it proposed to regard henceforth as an Iraqi province.

Months of diplomatic pressure failed to shift Saddam Hussein, even when it became clear that virtually the whole world was ranged against him. Only Jordan, (linked to Iraq by close ties of trade and kinship), as well as Yemen, Sudan and Libya expressed any sympathy for the Iraqi position.

A military alliance against Iraq, headed by the USA and Saudi Arabia, began to prepare for a massive operation against Iraq from Saudi territory. Britain, France and other European countries joined the international force, and from the Arab world Egypt, Syria and the Gulf states sent contingents of troops. But worst of all for

Saddam Hussein, he received no help at all from his traditional ally, the Soviet Union.

The UN imposed sanctions on Iraq and gave its backing to military action against it. The deadline for Iraq to withdraw expired on 15 January 1991. From 17 January, Allied aircraft bombarded Iraq, attacking military targets and Iraq's economic infrastructure of roads, factories and power supplies. The bombing was described by the Allies as precision bombing, but there were still civilian casualties.

Then on 24 February, after diplomatic efforts had failed to bring about a negotiated settlement, the USA and its allies launched the land war against the Iraqi forces to drive them out of Kuwait.

The process took only four days. Most of Iraq's army in Kuwait was destroyed and thousands of Iraqi troops were killed, many of them in the front lines as the US troops overran them, or in the so-called 'turkey shoot' when US aircraft destroyed large columns of fleeing Iraqi vehicles. On 28 February, President Bush of the USA ordered a cease-fire, and peace terms were agreed by Iraqi and Allied commanders on 3 March.

UN sanctions on Iraq were still in force in 1992, causing much suffering to the Iraqi people. Iraq was excluded from the world oil market, although it had formerly been a major producer, and the UN had not agreed on terms for export to begin again. Meanwhile, UN inspectors within Iraq found clear evidence that the country was at least some way towards acquiring a nuclear weapon. This would have made it the second nuclear state in the Middle East, since Israel is also known to have at least a hundred nuclear warheads and the ability to deliver them.

The USA did not press on, in March 1991, to destroy all Iraq's armed forces and did not try to bring about Saddam Hussein's downfall as a leader. But by 1992 the US government seemed to have decided that the downfall of Saddam Hussein was a desirable policy aim, and had begun to offer help to Iraqi opposition movements.

The land war in Kuwait was brought to a swift end when US aircraft annihilated long columns of vehicles retreating into Iraqi territory. Here, a US soldier surveys the wreckage.

CHAPTER 18

THE KURDS

I has been the plight of the Kurds in Iraq which has recently drawn the Kurds to the attention of the world, with tragic pictures of Kurdish refugees in the mountains of northern Iraq and southern Turkey.

But Iraq's Kurds are only a fraction of the total Kurdish population. There are 12 million Kurds in Turkey; and 4 million more in Syria, Iran and the Republic of Azerbaijan. Turkey in particular has always feared Kurdish separatism. The Kurds make up one-fifth of the population of Turkey, and there is a militant organization, the PKK (Kurdish Workers' Party) which wants a Kurdish state in Turkey.

After the First World War, when Kemal Ataturk's military and diplomatic success ensured that the Kurds did not get their own state in eastern Turkey, the Turks tried hard to suppress the Kurds. Their language was forbidden, and the Kurds were called 'mountain Turks'.

When the Iraqi government mounted a counter-offensive against the Kurds in March 1991, many Kurdish people left their homes and fled into the inhospitable mountain region of northern Iraq and southern Turkey.

The Kurdish province of Mosul was given to Iraq by the League of Nations in 1925 and the wishes of the Kurds were ignored. A Kurdish revolt in Turkey was crushed in 1928. This area is now the part of northern Iraq where, after severe persecution by the Iraqi government, the Kurds are again trying to set up an autonomous region. Only recently has there been some recognition of the existence of the Kurds in Turkey as a separate people.

It is not just in Turkey that the Kurds have failed consistently and tragically to achieve some political recognition. After the Second World War, in 1946, the Soviet Union gave its backing to a Kurdish state in Iranian territory, but this collapsed when Soviet forces withdrew. Iraq discussed autonomy with the Kurds in the early 1970s, and proposed a form of autonomy which the Kurds rejected in 1974 because it did not meet their demands.

After the end of the Gulf War, the Kurdish population in northern Iraq saw its chance to seize its freedom from the Iraqi state. In March 1991 the Kurds drove Iraqi troops out of the Kurdish area and took control of the towns. But the end of the Kurdish revolt came on 28 March 1991, when the Iraqi Army mounted its counter-offensive.

As Iraq's forces began once more to take control, the Kurds took refuge in the hills to escape retribution. With the example of the Iran–Iraq war before them, the Kurds feared massacres and indiscriminate attacks with good reason. In 1988, thousands of Kurdish civilians were killed by chemical weapons at the town of Halabja.

Of Iraq's population of over 3 million Kurds, hundreds of thousands fled their homes, taking refuge in the mountains. Up to a quarter of a million came to the Turkish border, but only a few were allowed to cross into Turkey. Others fled to Iran.

Effectively, the Kurdish uprising was over. However, the Western nations took some steps to protect the Kurds from the Iraqi armed forces. In April, forces of the Western coalition crossed into Iraq to mount a relief operation. In the following weeks the West encouraged Kurds to move out of the most inhospitable mountain regions into so-called 'safe havens' under Western protection.

Western air forces continued to protect the Kurds after the Western troops withdrew, and the Iraqis were forbidden to move against the Kurds on pain of renewed intervention.

In these circumstances, the leaders of the Kurds have tried to conduct talks with the government in Baghdad about autonomy for a Kurdish region. The leader of the Kurdish Democratic Party, Massoud Barzani, has headed Kurdish negotiations with Iraq. His rival, Jalal Talabani of the Patriotic Union of Kurdistan, has been less keen on talking to Saddam Hussein, though he also has made some contact with the Iraqi leader. In May 1992 elections for a Kurdish National Assembly were held, and there is now a Kurdish government although it is not recognized by Iraq.

If the Kurds were to succeed in gaining even limited autonomy in Iraq it would be a step towards creating the nation they have wanted for many years.

A survivor of Halabja tells his story:
'"My eyes became heavy, it hurt to breathe. I vomited eight or nine times." Muhammad Aziz is 25 years old. On March 16 he was at Halabja, in Iraqi Kurdistan, when the Iraqis attacked the village with mustard gas and nerve gas. A dreadful death toll ensued: five thousand dead and seven thousand wounded, according to the Iranian authorities. Muhammad was used to Iraqi attacks on his village, known as a Kurdish nationalist stronghold. But, sheltering in a cave, he immediately saw this attack was different. "We smelled the gas," he explained, coughing as he spoke. When he dared to go out after several hours he saw the streets littered with the bodies of the victims, dead and dying. "Every time I opened a door, there were men, women and children dying inside."'
(*Le Monde*, 8 April 1988.)

THE MIDDLE EAST PEACE TALKS

Intense pressure from the USA was the force that finally brought the Arabs and Israel together for talks about Middle East peace. The first session of the talks took place on 30 October 1991 in Madrid. After the Gulf War, the USA was determined to make an effort to bring comprehensive peace to the Middle East. President Bush was personally committed to the idea, and seemed more even-handed between the Israelis and the Arabs than previous presidents.

The first meeting of the delegations in Madrid was an historic occasion. Though not the first time Israelis and Arabs have negotiated about peace, it was the first time negotiators from Israel had officially met any kind of Palestinian delegation. Until then, Israel's tone had been that set by Mrs Golda Meir, prime minister during the 1973 October War. She always said that she would talk to any Arab leader about peace, but refused to admit even the existence of a separate Palestinian people.

A key factor was a change in Washington's attitude. Until 1991 the USA's commitment to Israel was unquestioned. A number of factors changed that. The 'Cold War' conflict between the capitalist West, led by the USA, and the communist East, led by the Soviet Union ended in the late 1980s. When the Soviet Union broke up in 1991, the USA became the world's most powerful country. So Israel's strategic importance (in standing up to Soviet interference in the Middle East) was reduced. Attitudes in the USA

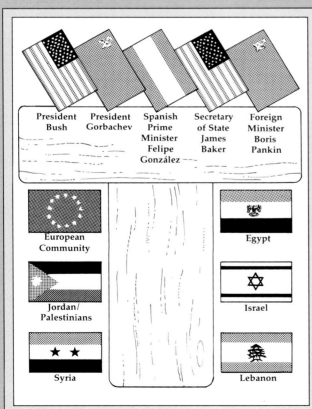

Participants in the Madrid peace conference.

Middle East peace conference, Madrid, Oct–Nov 1991
The main participants were:
The USA, represented by James Baker, the US Secretary of State. He had put together the conference, and his goal was to keep the Arabs and Israelis talking long enough to achieve some results.
The Soviet Union was supposedly an equal partner with the USA, but had too many domestic problems to play an important role.
Yitzhak Shamir, the Israeli Prime Minister, who would not compromise easily on the land-for-peace issue.
The Palestinian delegation, run by the PLO. Faisal al-Husseini, who was widely described as the real leader of the Palestinian delegation, was banned from the negotiating table (because the Israelis regarded him as living in Israel itself rather than the Occupied Territories).
Jordan, which faced the biggest problem at home, because of bitter Muslim fundamentalist opposition to the talks.
Syria, which has fought four wars with Israel, remains its main enemy. In reality, it has little love for the mainstream PLO.
Egypt, Lebanon and the European Community were also represented.

ISRAEL WANTS PEACE

A large demonstration of over 50,000 Israelis calling for peace gathered in Tel Aviv on the eve of the Madrid conference. It was an indication of political changes in Israel in recent years.

towards Israel have changed during the *intifada*, as Israel began to seem oppressive towards the Palestinians. Finally, US politicians seem less impressed by Israeli lobbying organizations in Washington.

Israel was nevertheless allowed to set conditions for the talks. Israel has always rejected the idea of negotiations with the Palestine Liberation Organization, which it says is dedicated to the destruction of Israel. But the Israeli government agreed to talk to a Palestinian delegation representing the Palestinians who live in the Occupied Territories of Gaza and the West Bank.

Israel has also always been reluctant to agree to a multilateral conference on Middle East peace, especially if states outside the region were involved. The Arabs therefore agreed to hold bilateral talks with Israel, where each Arab delegation would talk separately to the Israelis.

By June 1992, when Israel's general election was held, five rounds of bilateral talks had taken place, as well as several multilateral meetings to discuss general issues of regional importance. Members of the Palestinian delegation reported that Israel seemed unwilling to discuss matters of substance ahead of the election, but nevertheless the Palestinians believed it was important to keep the talks going.

In the June election in Israel, the right-wing Likud Block, which had been in power in Israel since 1977, lost its majority, and a new government was formed by the Labour Party. Yitzhak Rabin, a former Israeli chief of staff, defence minister and prime minister, returned to power. Labour's plans included the aim of reaching early agreement with the Palestinians on some form of autonomy within the Occupied Territories. With Labour in power, the talks showed a chance of bearing more fruit than had originally been hoped for.

43

CHAPTER 20

CONCLUSION

The 1990s has been a period of rapid change in the Middle East. The opening of the Middle East peace talks raised hopes that a solution could be found to the Arab–Israeli issue, which has been at the heart of the instability of the region since 1948. The apparent settlement of Lebanon's sixteen-year civil war in 1991 showed that fear of further bloodshed had triumphed (for the time being) over the belief that disagreements can be settled by violence.

A Palestinian from a camp in Lebanon shows her misery at the constant killing and destruction.

Elsewhere in the region, the Gulf War mobilized a million soldiers but proved that in the post-Cold War era, a war to achieve a limited and apparently just aim can be fought without dragging the world into a wider conflict. But the Gulf War also raised the alarming prospect that the USA, after the demise of the Soviet Union as a world power, has no brake on its ability to intervene in disputes between other countries.

In 1992, problems in the Middle East still loomed large. Israel's new Labour government looked more amenable to negotiation with the Palestinians than its predecessors, but this remained untried in practice. Lebanon could still revert to violence, especially if the grievances of the poorest community, the Shi'ite third of the country, remain unaddressed.

In Iraq, Saddam Hussein was still in power, while Iraq's Shi'ite and Kurdish peoples were

In the aftermath of the Gulf War, a victorious Allied soldier guards a pile of weapons confiscated from defeated Iraqi soldiers. Iraq's defeat reduced the chances of large-scale armed conflict in the Middle East at least in the short term.

trying to decide how to unseat him. The Gulf states had not yet decided how to assure their future security. There was still the possibility that future disturbances of some kind might disrupt the flow of oil from the Gulf to Western consumers. Iran had not yet clarified how far it wanted to press its claim to be consulted over security in the Gulf. And the pressure of ordinary people to be heard in government, increasingly expressed through the channel of what is seen in the West as Islamic fundamentalism, is growing steadily.

Whether the Middle East will be the scene of more conflict in the remainder of the twentieth century, either through the resurgence of one of the existing issues or through the outbreak of some new and unforeseen crisis, cannot be guessed. What is certain is that the Middle East will not cease to be a focus of attention in world affairs.

An ordinary day in a busy Cairo street. Although many Middle Eastern countries have suffered much conflict, in most cities normal life continues.

45

GLOSSARY

Alawi A religious sect in Syria, whose beliefs differ slightly from those of ordinary Muslims. The President of Syria, Hafez al-Assad, is an Alawi, and members of the sect play an important part in governing the country.

Arab League The Arab League is an international organization of Arab states. It was formed in 1945 to provide an international forum for joint decisions to be made by Arab states and for the discussion between them of international problems.

Azerbaijan A Muslim state which was a member of the former Soviet Union. It has borders with Turkey and Iran.

Ba'ath Means 'rebirth', and is the name of a political philosophy and a political party founded by a group of Syrian intellectuals in the 1930s. It teaches a socialist political philosophy combined with the ideal of political unity for all the Arabs. It is the official political doctrine in both Syria and Iraq.

Bilateral Something done by, or affecting, two countries or parties. See also Multilateral.

Druze A religious sect in Lebanon, whose beliefs are connected to those of Islam but are not exactly the same. The Druze also have their own militia and political party. Their leader Walid Jumblatt is strongly left-wing.

Fundamentalist Someone who believes in returning to and practising the fundamental beliefs of religion, with no modern interpretation. Muslim fundamentalists in general reject the word, and say they are simply good Muslims.

Golan Heights A mountainous area of Syria, overlooking the north of Israel, captured by Israel in the war of June 1967 and annexed by Israel in 1981.

Gulf Known as the Persian Gulf (by Iran) and Arabian Gulf (by the Arabs), the Gulf is the sea between the Arabian Peninsula to the west and Iran to the east.

Gulf States These are Kuwait, Bahrain, Qatar, the United Arab Emirates, Saudi Arabia and Oman. They each have a coastline on the Gulf, and are all members of the Gulf Co-operation Council.

Hashemite The sons of Hussein ibn Ali al-Hashemi, the Sherif (or governor) of Mecca at the time of the First World War, were called Hashemites. They fought on the British side and were rewarded with Arabian Kingdoms by the British government. Faisal became King of Iraq and Abdullah ruled Jordan. King Hussein of Jordan is the last remaining Hashemite monarch.

Hizbollah A Shi'ite political faction in south Lebanon, which is supported by Iran. It is strongly militant, and opposes both Israel and the Christian-dominated Lebanese government.

Intifada The Palestinian uprising, which began in December 1987. In Arabic, it means literally a 'shaking up'. The word is a metaphor: its literal meaning is when the branches of an olive tree are shaken to bring down fruit.

Kurdistan What the Kurds call the region where they live. It would also be the name of the independent state the Kurds want to set up, if it ever came into being.

Maronite A Christian sect found in Lebanon. The Maronite community has traditionally been dominant in Lebanon.

Militia An unofficial armed organization. Most political movements in Lebanon had a militia during the civil war.

Mufti The Mufti of a town or region is a Muslim cleric recognized by his colleagues as qualified to give definitive answers to questions about the interpretation of Islam. An opinion given by a Mufti is known as a *Fatwa*.

Multilateral Something done by, or affecting, more than two countries or parties. 'Multilateral talks' means negotiations involving three or more organizations, countries etc.

Muslim Brotherhood One of the main fundamentalist Muslim movements. It was begun in Egypt in the 1920s by Hassan al-Banna. Today it is represented in many Arab countries, especially Jordan where it has some political strength. In some other countries it is banned or discouraged. Its followers are mainly Sunni Muslims.

OAPEC The 'Organization of Arab Petroleum Exporting Countries', formed by Arab members of OPEC in 1968.

Occupied Territories The areas of the West Bank of the River Jordan, including East Jerusalem, and the Gaza Strip in south-west Israel, which were left under Arab administration in 1948 but were occupied by Israel in 1967.

OPEC Means 'Organization of Petroleum Exporting Countries'. Founded in 1960. All the Arab oil-producing countries are members, except Oman.

PLO The Palestine Liberation Organization which was founded in 1964. Today it is an organization which includes all the Palestinian guerrilla groups. The leader of the PLO is its chairman, Yasser Arafat, who is also leader of Fatah, the biggest guerrilla group.

Sanctions Restrictions on trade or other activities imposed on one state or organization by another.

Shi'ite A faction of Muslims which split off from the main body of Islam in the early days of the religion. They believe that there is a 'hidden Imam' in the world who leads the faith (though we may not know who he is). They have different traditions and they sometimes express their beliefs more strongly than other Muslim sects.

Sunni Sunni Muslims are orthodox Muslims, who base their religion on the Sunna (what Muhammad did), the Qur'an, and the Hadith (traditions about what Muhammad said). They make up 90 per cent of Muslims today.

UN The United Nations is the international organization which was formed in 1945 with the principal aim of maintaining world peace. All sovereign states have the right to membership. All members participate in the General Assembly, and fifteen are members of the Security Council.

UN Security Council The decision-making body of the United Nations. It has fifteen members of whom five are permanent, namely the USA, Russia, France, Britain and China. The other ten members are chosen on a rotating basis from the membership of the United Nations for fixed periods. Its decisions are taken by a simple majority vote, but any permanent member may veto a decision. Resolutions are not binding but have a strong moral force over UN members.

Wahhabi The Saudi ruling family adheres to the teachings of the Wahhabis, who were a puritanical Islamic sect in Arabia in the eighteenth century, led by Muhammad ibn Abdul Wahhab.

Zionist Zionism is the belief that the Jewish people should have a country of their own. Zionism now implies support for the State of Israel. The word comes from the hill on which the city of Jerusalem stands – Zion.

FURTHER INFORMATION

Newspapers and reference
The serious newspapers cover Middle Eastern news extensively. Larger reference libraries always have *Keesing's Record of World Events* where past events can be looked up in great detail. *The Middle East and North Africa*, published annually by Europa, gives a wealth of information. A more concise book published in 1991 is *The Times Guide to the Middle East.*

General reading
Childs, Nick   *The Gulf War* (Wayland, 1988). Covers the 1980–88 Iran–Iraq War.
Gresh, Alain and Vidal, Dominique   *A to Z of the Middle East* (Zed Books, 1990)
Harper, Paul   *The Arab–Israeli Conflict* (Wayland, 1989)
King, John   *The Gulf War* (Wayland, 1991). Covers the 1990–91 Iraq–Kuwait conflict.
Mansfield, Peter   *A History of the Middle East* (Penguin, 1992)

More advanced books
Fisk, Robert   *Pity the Nation: Lebanon at War* (OUP, 1992)
Friedman, Thomas   *From Beirut to Jerusalem* (Fontana, 1990)
Hourani, Albert   *A History of the Arab Peoples* (Faber, 1992)
Kyle, Keith   *Suez* (Weidenfeld, 1992)
Seale, Patrick   *Asad of Syria* (Tauris, 1988)

The Gulf War
Bulloch, John and Morris, Harvey   *Saddam's War* (Faber, 1991)
Heikal, Mohammed   *Illusions of Triumph: Arab View of the Gulf War* (Harper Collins, 1992)
Simpson, John   *From the House of War* (Arrow, 1991)
Stanwood, Frederick   *Gulf War: a day by day chronicle* (Octopus, 1991)

Arab–Israeli Conflict
Ovendale, Ritchie   *The Origins of the Arab–Israeli Wars* (Longman, 1992)

Intifada
Bennis, Phyllis and Cassidy, Neal   *From Stones to Statehood: Palestinian Uprising* (Zed Books, 1990)
McDowall, David   *Palestine and Israel: the Uprising and Beyond* (Tauris, 1990)

PLO
Wallach, John and Janet   *Arafat* (Mandarin, 1992)

Kurds
Bullock, John and Morris, Harvey   *No Friends but the Mountains* (Viking, 1992)
King, John   *The Kurds*   (Wayland, 1993)
McDowall, David   *The Kurds* (Minority Rights Group, 1991)

Novels
There is a wealth of literature written in, or about, the Middle East. Novels with a modern setting include *Eight Months on Ghazzah Street* by Hilary Mantel (Penguin, 1989), about a foreign woman in Saudi Arabia; and two books by Nawal el Sa'dawi, an Egyptian feminist writer: *Two Women in One* (Al Saqi Books, 1985), the story of an 18-year-old medical student in Cairo, and *The Fall of the Imam* (Minerva, 1989), a fantasy directed against Islamic fundamentalism.

There are several novels about life in Egypt before or at the time of the Egyptian revolution: *Midaq Alley* by Najib Mahfuz, a recent Nobel Prize Winner (Doubleday, 1992), and Waguih Ghali's *Beer in the Snooker Club* (Serpent's Tail, 1987).

Two books set in Israel are by Amos Oz: *My Michael*, set in the 1950s, and *Black Box*, a family history in the 1980s.

Elias Khoury's *Little Mountain* describes the experiences of a guerrilla fighter in the Lebanese civil war (Collins Harvill, 1990).

Nisanit, by Fadia Faqir (Adrian Ellis, 1987) and *The Secret Life of Saeed* by Emile Habiby (Zed Books, 1985) are both fantasies set in occupied Palestine.

Films
Probably the best-known film set in the Middle East is *Lawrence of Arabia*, a Western account of T.E.Lawrence and the Arab revolt.

The Egyptian film-maker Yusuf Shahine is notable for two films: *Alexandria Why?*, about events in Egypt during the Second World War, and *Alexandria Now and Forever*, set in contemporary Egypt. Another famous Egyptian film is *The Night of Counting the Years* which looks at the moral dilemmas of a poverty-stricken community.

Hamsin, a film made in Israel, is set in a small farming village in northern Israel, when people become suspicious that the government intends to take the local Arab lands. The consequent bitterness and hostility destroys old Arab-Jewish friendships and loyalties.

An Iranian film, *The Runner*, deals with an illiterate ten-year-old orphan struggling to survive in a shanty town on the Persian Gulf. It has been described as 'an astonishing piece of film-making'.

INDEX

Abu Nidal   23, 25
Arab
  Christians   9, 28
  –Israeli Wars:
  (1948)   15
  (1967)   8, 15, 19, 20-1
  (1973)   see October War
  language   9, 34
  League   27, 46
  nationalism   12-13
  people   6, 8, 10, 14-15, 18, 23, 27, 42-3
Arafat, Yasser   24
Assad, President   33, 46
Aswan High Dam   17
Ataturk, Mustafa   10, 40
autocracy   7

Ba'ath Party   7, 13, 32-3, 46
Baghdad Pact   13
Balfour Declaration   10-11, 14
Ben-Gurion, David   14, 16
Britain   10, 11, 12-13, 16, 22, 24, 38

chemical weapons   34, 41
climate   7
Copts   9

democracy   5, 7, 8, 30
desert   7
Druzes   28, 46

Egypt   5, 6, 7, 8, 9, 11, 12, 13, 15, 16-17, 20-1, 22-3, 26-7, 32, 38, 42
El Alamein, battle of   12

fertile land   7
First World War   10-11, 34, 40
France   10, 12, 13, 16, 22, 38
Free French   10, 12

Gaddafi, Colonel   22-3
Gaza strip   15, 36, 43
Germany   10, 12-13, 14
Gulf States   7, 8, 11, 38, 45, 46
Gulf War   4, 8, 9, 33, 35, 38-9, 41, 42, 43

Hashemites   10, 46
Hizbollah   29, 46
hostages   29, 30
Hussein, Saddam   32-3, 34-5, 38-9, 44

intifada   36-7, 43, 46
Iran   4, 7, 9, 10, 11, 13, 19, 29, 30-1, 34-5, 40, 45
  -Iraq War   8, 30, 33, 34-5
Iraq   4, 6, 7, 8, 9, 11, 13, 18, 19, 25, 32-3, 34-5, 38-9, 40-1, 44, 46
Islam   9, 28, 30-1
Islamic republic   11
Israel   4, 5, 6, 8, 9, 10, 14-15, 16, 20-1, 24, 26-7, 28, 36,-7, 39, 42-3, 44
Italy   11, 12, 22
Jamahiriyyah   7
Jews   8, 9, 10, 11, 14-15
Jordan   6, 7, 10, 13, 15, 20-1, 24, 38-9

Khomeini, Ayatollah   8, 30-1
King Farouk   11, 16
King Hussein   10, 20, 24, 46
King Idris   22
Kurdistan   11, 46
Kurds   7, 11, 32, 40-1, 44
Kuwait   4, 5, 19, 38-9

Lawrence of Arabia   10
League of Nations   10, 40
Lebanon   6, 7, 9, 10, 28-9, 42, 44
Libya   7, 8, 11, 12, 19, 22-3, 25, 38
Lockerbie bombing   23

Middle East Peace Talks   4, 42-3, 44
modernization   5, 30
monarchy   7
Muslim   8, 28
  Alawi   33, 46
  Brotherhood   12, 33, 46
  Fundamentalism   5, 12, 27, 30, 45, 46
  Shi'ite   9, 28, 29, 30, 32, 34, 44, 46
  Sunni   9, 13, 28, 32, 46

Nasser, President   8, 11, 13, 16-17, 21, 22, 26
nuclear weapons   39

OAPEC   19, 46
Occupied Territories   8, 37, 43, 46
October War (1973)   19, 26-7
oil   4, 5, 8, 18-19, 22, 34, 45

OPEC   18-19, 46
Ottoman Empire   6, 10,11

Palestine   4, 6, 10, 11, 13, 14-15, 25
Palestinians   4, 10, 23, 24-5, 28, 36-7, 42-3, 44
Paris peace conference   10
PFLP   24-5
PLO   24-5, 29, 42, 43, 46

Qur'an   9

refugees   15, 28, 40-1
religion   5, 9

Sadat, President   13, 26-7
San Remo conference   10,11
Saudi Arabia   5, 7, 11, 18, 19, 29, 38-9
Second World War   10, 11, 12-13, 15, 22, 40
Shah (of Iran)   8, 11, 30
Sinai   16, 20-1, 26-7
Soviet Muslim Republics   8, 9, 46
Soviet Union   7, 13, 17, 19, 26, 30, 39, 40-1, 42-3, 44
Suez Canal   16-17, 21, 26, 27
Syria   6, 7, 9, 10, 13, 20-1, 28, 33, 38, 40, 42, 46

terrorism   23, 24-5
theocracy   8
Turkey   6, 7, 8, 9, 10, 11, 13, 40

United Nations   15, 21, 24, 28, 35, 38-9, 47
USA   4, 13, 16, 17, 18, 22, 23, 26-7, 30, 35, 38-9, 42-3, 44
  aid   8

Vichy regime   12

Wahhabis   11, 47
water   5
West Bank   21, 24, 36, 43

Yemen   8, 11, 38

Zionist   10, 11, 14-15, 47